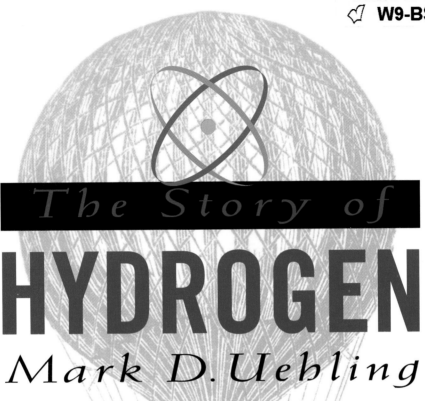

The Story of

HYDROGEN

Mark D. Uebling

A FIRST BOOK

FRANKLIN WATTS
A Division of Grolier Publishing
New York London Hong Kong Sydney
Danbury, Connecticut

Cover design by Robin Hessel Hoffmann

Photographs copyright ©: National Air and Space Museum, The Smithsonian
Institution: pp. 6 (A4201 B-1), 19 (76-1196), 20 (A 30915 H), North Wind
Picture Archive: pp. 7, 15; Fundamental Photographs: pp. 10 (Richard Megna),
36 (Jack Plekan); The Bettmann Archive: pp. 11, 24, 26; Photo Researchers,
Inc.: pp. 13 (Michael P. Godomski), 27 (Ken Eward/SS), 29 (CERN/P.
Loiez/SPL), 31 (Ken Eward/SS) 39 (Ken Eward/SS), 40 (S.J. Krasemann/NAS);
UPI/Bettmann: p. 22; Sandia National Laboratories, Livermore, CA.: p. 46;
NASA: p. 48; U.S. Department of Energy: pp. 50, 51; Los Alamos National
Laboratory: pp. 53,55.

Library of Congress Cataloging-in-Publication Data
Uehling, Mark.
     The story of hydrogen/by Mark Uehling.
        p.   cm. — (A First Book)
     Includes bibliographical references (p. —) and index.
     Summary: Discusses the discovery, nature, behavior, and uses of the
element hydrogen.
     ISBN 0-531-20213-5
     1. Hydrogen—Juvenile literature. [1. Hydrogen.] I. Title.
II. Series.
QD181.H1U34   1995
546'.2—dc20   95-9543
                                        CIP   AC

Contents

THE LITTLE GHOST

Before there were planes, the only way people could fly was in balloons. Balloons were the first to take passengers on long trips high above the ground into the sky. And we have hydrogen to thank for that.

Hydrogen is a *gas* that fills up balloons like air does. It looks just like air, but it is different. Hydrogen weighs less than any other substance on earth. It may sound strange, but its light weight gives it the power to lift very heavy weights into the air. Hydrogen rises because it is fifteen times lighter than air.

The very first balloons that people tried to fly were filled with hot air. Hot air rises too. But these balloons couldn't stay up for very long because passengers had to keep burning wool and straw so that the air would stay hot—and light. That was in 1783.

That same year a French physicist named Jacques Charles got the bright idea to fill his balloon with hydrogen. He knew that this wonderful gas is lighter than air

Jacques Charles and his friend take off from Paris in 1783 with the help of hydrogen.

whether it's hot or not. Hydrogen took Charles and a friend of his on an astounding two-hour flight that thrilled the people in the fields below. Charles said peasants ran after the balloon like children chasing a butterfly.

Most people at that time had never heard of hydrogen and had no idea that balloons could fly. When a hydrogen balloon came floating into a field from far away one day, some French farmers were so frightened that they shredded it with their pitchforks. They had never seen anything like it.

Frightened French farmers stabbed a hydrogen balloon with their pitchforks.

7

Scientists had discovered hydrogen only a few years before the balloonists began using it. One of the first remarkable things they found about hydrogen was that, besides being so light, it was able to create drops of water! All they had to do was mix hydrogen with air and add a spark. After an explosion, water would appear.

Hydrogen seemed very mysterious because it is invisible. You cannot feel it or taste it or smell it. It is like a little ghost that is in the air but you don't know it's there. That's why scientists took so long to discover it.

But in the 200 years since its discovery, scientists have gotten to know this little ghost very well. They learned that it is very, very old—as old as the stars themselves. Hydrogen is the fuel that makes the Sun and the stars shine.

As you read on, you will get to know hydrogen, too. You'll find that it has many talents that have helped people immensely. You'll also find that, at times, it has caused terrible tragedy. Depending on how it is used, its powers can be dangerous and scary. You will learn much of what scientists know about hydrogen and all the ways that it has affected our lives. This is the story of hydrogen.

Chapter 2

THE DISCOVERY OF HYDROGEN

Finding hydrogen was not easy. When scientists aren't aware that something exists, it's difficult to look for it! In the 1600s, several scientists came upon hydrogen accidentally while they were experimenting in their laboratories, but they didn't realize what it was.

At that time, scientists didn't even know there was such a thing as gases. They knew that air exists, but they didn't realize that it is a mixture of many gases, including *nitrogen* and *oxygen*.

Among the first to notice hydrogen was an English chemist named Robert Boyle. One day in 1671, he mixed pieces of iron with some acid. The metal pieces began dancing and sizzling as if they were being cooked in the

Robert Boyle added metal filings to some acid,
and the little ghost appeared!

acid. Fumes rose from the metal pieces as they dissolved. Those fumes were none other than the little ghost appearing before his eyes.

But Boyle didn't know what the fumes were, so he tried bringing a lit candle to them. They immediately caught fire and burned with a greenish-blue flame. He was fascinated by this burning gas, but he never found out what it was.

A century later, in 1766, an English chemist named Henry Cavendish tried similar experiments with iron, zinc, and copper. All three metals gave off the same fumes when they were combined with acid. He captured the rising fumes in a bottle and weighed them.

When Cavendish saw that the gas was much lighter than air, he realized that it was a new substance. Because

Henry Cavendish discovered hydrogen in 1766.

it went up in flames so easily, he called it "inflammable air." At last, someone recognized that the little ghost existed!

Joseph Priestley, an English chemist who knew Cavendish well, soon discovered other gases. He ran many tests on these gases, including hydrogen. One day in 1781, he shot an electric spark into a bottle of hydrogen mixed with some air. There was an explosion inside the bottle!

Afterward, he noticed something like dew on the inside walls of the bottle. When Cavendish heard about this experiment, he tried it himself. He found that after the explosion, all that remained was a little air and some drops of water. Then he tried mixing hydrogen and oxygen, another gas Priestley had recently discovered in the air. This mixture exploded too, and all the gas in the bottle changed into water.

SOLVING THE MYSTERY

When a French chemist named Antoine Lavoisier heard the news of Cavendish's experiment, he became very excited. He was pretty sure he knew what was happening inside the bottle. He had already done many experiments with water to find out whether it was one of the earth's *elements*, as most people believed at that time.

In fact, people had believed water was an element for more than 2,000 years. The ancient Greeks came up with the idea of elements after wondering about what things

Antoine Lavoisier was fascinated by water. He wanted to find out if it was one of the elements that make up everything on earth.

are made of. They thought there must be some basic substances, or elements, that make up everything on earth. The question was, what were these elements?

A Greek thinker named Empedocles proposed that there were four elements. He thought that everything was made of earth, air, fire, and water. The idea became popular after the Greek philosopher Aristotle agreed with him. Long after Aristotle's time, people continued to believe it because there was no way to test it.

In the eighteenth century Lavoisier and other scientists began to doubt Empedocles's theory. They tried to find ways to test whether earth, air, water, and fire were really elements. If they could show that any of the four was made of other substances, they reasoned, then it couldn't be an element.

Lavoisier did many experiments to see whether water could be broken down into parts. When he heard about Cavendish's experiment, he immediately suspected that hydrogen and oxygen were the parts of water. He rushed to do his own experiments with the two gases.

Just as Cavendish had done, Lavoisier made water from the two gases. He was convinced then that the two gases were the parts of water. But it took longer to convince other scientists. It must have been hard for them to believe that a liquid you can see and feel could be made of two invisible gases. They did not really accept it until Lavoisier found a way to change water into hydrogen and oxygen.

After his experiments, Lavoisier had no doubt that the gases were completely new substances—not just different forms of air. So Lavoisier renamed them, just as parents might name their babies. Inflammable air became *hydrogen*, which means "watermaker" in Greek, and the other gas became *oxygen*.

To make water, hydrogen and oxygen must undergo a *chemical reaction*. The reaction between hydrogen and oxygen can be started by either a spark or by fire. When hydrogen burns, it is really combining with oxygen in the air to form water.

Lavoisier did many experiments with gases in his laboratory.

Lavoisier was the first person to realize that whenever anything burns in air, it is reacting chemically with oxygen to form a *compound*. A compound is a material made up of more than one element. It is different from a mixture, such as lemonade. In a mixture, the ingredients mingle with each other but do not react with each other. A mixture has many of the same qualities as its ingredients, but a compound is usually very different from its elements.

Another example of a chemical reaction is the one that Boyle and Cavendish saw when they combined metal and acid. Acid is a compound containing hydrogen. When the metal was added, the acid broke down into its elements, and the hydrogen was free to float away in its ghostly form. The metal, an element itself, combined with another element in the acid, forming a powder.

Lavoisier's discovery had a great impact on chemistry. It eventually caused scientists to throw out the four-element theory once and for all. Lavoisier convinced them that hydrogen and oxygen are the true elements—not earth, air, water, or fire. He also recognized that many other substances, such as aluminum, zinc, and nickel, are elements. Over time, scientists discovered a total of ninety-two elements in nature, and generated more artificially in laboratories.

Lavoisier put scientists on the right path to the true elements. Because of this, he is known as the father of modern chemistry. And hydrogen was one of his firstborn.

Chapter 3

LIGHTER THAN AIR

Scientists were very curious about the invisible gases that Lavoisier had discovered. Just as you might spend hours with a new toy or pet discovering what it's like and all the ways you can have fun with it, scientists ran many experiments to find out what hydrogen is like. They wanted to know how it behaves and all the ways it could be useful to people.

Of course, one of the first things Cavendish had noticed was how light hydrogen is. He saw this by weighing some hydrogen in a bottle and subtracting the weight of the bottle. Then he calculated hydrogen's *density* by dividing its weight by the amount of space inside the bottle—its *volume*. When he compared this number to the densities of other materials, he found that hydrogen had the smallest density of all. Hydrogen's density is so little that 1,333 gallons (5,045 liters) of hydrogen—about a whole roomful—weighs only 1 pound (about ½ kg)!

Jacques Charles knew about Cavendish's amazing finding when he began designing his flying balloon in 1783. He realized that, because hydrogen is so light, it would lift a balloon much more easily than hot air. A balloon filled with hydrogen would rise through the air as a bubble of air rises through water. Just as air is less dense than water, hydrogen is less dense than air.

The only problem was collecting enough hydrogen to fill a balloon. That's when Lavoisier found a way to break water down into hydrogen and oxygen. He was trying to help make hydrogen balloons practical for flying and other purposes.

HYDROGEN TAKES OFF

Very soon after the great success of the first balloon flights, it occurred to some people that balloons could be very useful in fighting wars. If the balloons were tied to one spot over the ground, they could serve as very high lookout posts from which to watch for the enemy. In 1793, the French government began studying ways to produce hydrogen for such balloons. The following year France created the world's first air force, and it was based on hydrogen balloons.

One of the first uses of hydrogen balloons was as lookout posts during battles, such as the one shown here between France and Austria in 1794.

Military balloons were used in the French Revolution and in the wars that the French emperor Napoleon fought in the early 1800s. The United States began using them during the Civil War, in 1861. Yankee scouts stayed up in the balloons for as long as two weeks watching troop movements on the Confederate side.

One of the officers who went up in the balloons was the son of a German count. He had come to the United States in 1863 to offer President Lincoln his help in fighting the war. His name was Count Ferdinand von Zeppelin. He was so impressed by the balloons that in 1891 he set

This Yankee soldier is going up in a hydrogen balloon to watch for Confederate soldiers during the Civil War.

out to design one that would move through the air the way a ship moves through water. Such an airship would be able to take passengers quickly over long distances.

French engineers had already been experimenting with adding engines to hydrogen balloons so that they could be steered and propelled forward. They designed balloons called *dirigibles*, airships that were shaped like cigars so they could move through the air more easily.

Count von Zeppelin built much larger dirigibles that were shaped more like ships than cigars. An aluminum frame underneath the balloon fabric made it strong and rigid. Germany used these dirigibles, which were called *zeppelins*, during World War I to drop bombs on England. The German military had only a few zeppelins at the beginning of the war, but by the end of it they had 88.

In 1910, a company formed by the count began taking people on luxury trips in zeppelins to various destinations. By 1929, they were crossing the Atlantic Ocean, and eventually they traveled between Europe and South America. The little ghost had ushered in the age of international air travel.

But hydrogen's glory days did not last long. One of the company's airships was called the *Hindenburg*. Made of lightweight aluminum, it was 810 feet (247 meters) long and flew at 80 miles per hour (130 kph)—faster than cars are allowed to drive today. Like a luxury ocean liner, it had lounges, a library, and a grand piano. During 1936, the *Hindenburg* safely flew 1,200 passengers between the United States and Germany. They were able to cross the

The Hindenburg, *a zeppelin filled with hydrogen, flew over New York City in 1937. Passengers rode in the belly of the balloon behind the small compartment.*

Atlantic Ocean in only a few days, which was a much shorter time than it took to go by ship.

By May 1937, the *Hindenburg* had crossed the ocean 20 times. That's when tragedy struck. As the *Hindenburg* was about to dock near Lakehurst, New Jersey, it caught fire. No one knows what started it. The zeppelin may have been flying too low and may have hit an electric tower. Or someone wanting to destroy the airship may have set the fire on purpose. Or a spark from an electrostatic charge in the air after a recent thunderstorm may have started the fire.

Not long after the fire started, the hydrogen exploded in a great ball of fire that rose above the ship. In less than a minute, the hydrogen was replaced with clouds of *water vapor*, or steam, hanging in the air. Thirty-five of the ninety-seven people on board died, along with another person on the ground.

The burning hydrogen had combined with oxygen in the air, making water vapor. This was the same chemical reaction Lavoisier discovered. Ever since Cavendish experimented with hydrogen, scientists knew it could catch fire very easily. Some people say the Germans should have known that hydrogen is too dangerous for passenger air travel. Other countries had realized it and stopped using it in dirigibles before the *Hindenburg* blew up. They used another invisible gas, called *helium*, which had recently been discovered. In fact, the Germans had wanted to switch to helium, too, but it was so scarce at that time that they couldn't get any.

Even though helium is safe, people were too terrified to travel in dirigibles after the *Hindenburg* disaster. The time of the elegant, luxurious airships had ended. Today helium, not hydrogen, is used in the blimps that float through the sky advertising products and companies, such as Goodyear.

The last flight of the Hindenburg *ended in disaster. When the hydrogen inside caught fire, the zeppelin exploded in a ball of flames.*

GETTING TO KNOW HYDROGEN

Helium is a very light element, but not as light as hydrogen. Since the discovery of hydrogen, scientists have not been able to find any element with a lower density. From the time the first known elements were organized by weight, hydrogen has reigned supreme as number 1. The reason it is so light gradually became clear in the nineteenth century.

Not long after hydrogen and oxygen were discovered, the English chemist John Dalton began to understand what gives elements their density and other *properties*. Properties are an element's characteristics—what it is like and how it behaves. Elements—and compounds, too—tend to act the same way all the time. You may have a dog who always jumps up and down excitedly when you come home. Similarly, in normal air, water always freezes at $32\,^{\circ}F$ ($0\,^{\circ}C$) and boils at $212\,^{\circ}F$ ($100\,^{\circ}C$). And hydrogen always has the same very low density.

Dalton realized that elements and compounds are made up of particles called atoms. If you kept dividing an element into smaller and smaller pieces, you'd eventually end up with a single atom. Although these atoms are much too tiny to see, Dalton knew they must be there because of the way elements combine with each other to form compounds. He also figured out that the atoms of one element have a different size and weight than the atoms of other elements. That must be why, he guessed, elements act different from each other. The fact that each element

ELEMENTS

		w.t			w.t
⊙	Hydrogen.	1	⊕	Strontian	46
⊖	Azote	5	⊛	Barytes	68
●	Carbon	5	Ⓘ	Iron	50
○	Oxygen	7	Ⓩ	Zinc	56
⊘	Phosphorus	9	Ⓒ	Copper	56
⊕	Sulphur	13	Ⓛ	Lead	90
⊗	Magnesia	20	Ⓢ	Silver	190
⊖	Lime	24	Ⓖ	Gold	190
⊕	Soda	28	Ⓟ	Platina	190
⊕	Potash	42	⊛	Mercury	167

John Dalton listed all the substances he believed were elements in 1803. He gave their weights compared to hydrogen, which he marked as weighing "1."

is made up of only one kind of atom makes elements basic substances.

When elements form compounds, their atoms cling together in identical groups called *molecules*. Water, for example, is a compound made up of molecules containing

A computer made this picture of water molecules spreading apart as they evaporate. The blue balls are oxygen atoms and the purple balls are hydrogen atoms.

two hydrogen atoms and one oxygen atom. That's why it's called H_2O. H is the chemical symbol for hydrogen, and O is the symbol for oxygen.

Molecules also exist in pure elements, such as hydrogen and other gases. Hydrogen atoms cling together in pairs, as if they don't like being alone. Because of this, a molecule of the element hydrogen is called H_2.

These hydrogen molecules are far away from one another, just as the particles of all gases are. When water boils and becomes a gas called water vapor, its molecules move farther apart as they rise into the air. The heat gives the molecules of the liquid the energy to speed up and rise into the air as a gas. When water freezes into ice, its molecules slow down and move closer together.

Hydrogen molecules move through space faster than the particles of any other gas. This high speed is another property of hydrogen. Cooling the gas slows the molecules down and moves them closer together. But the molecules are moving so fast that hydrogen must be cooled to -423°F (-253°C) before it becomes a liquid. To become solid like ice, it must be cooled to -452°F (-269°C). That's only 8 degrees F (4 degrees C) above *absolute zero*—the lowest temperature possible!

Because hydrogen is so light and its molecules move so fast, it makes up only a tiny fraction of a percent of air. Hydrogen molecules tend to rise to the top of the atmosphere and fly off into outer space. As you will find in Chapter 5, outer space is where most of the hydrogen in the universe resides.

WHAT MAKES HYDROGEN SO LIGHT

Even after they heard what Dalton had to say, many scientists in the 1800s did not believe atoms existed. It took the discovery of the *electron* early in this century to prove that atoms are real. Scientists first came across electrons in electricity, and then found that they're inside atoms, too.

An electron is a tiny particle with a negative electric

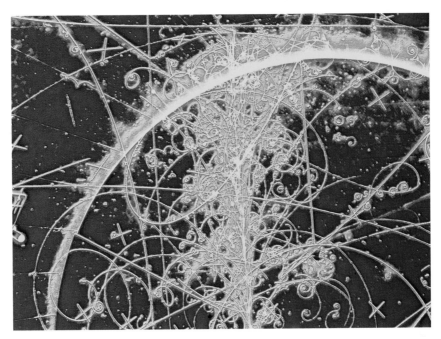

Although no one has really seen electrons, scientists can see the tracks they and other particles leave in a bubble chamber. The tight spirals you see in this photograph are the tracks of electrons. Liquid hydrogen in a bubble chamber makes the tracks visible.

charge. Another particle inside atoms, a *proton*, has a positive electric charge. These opposite charges attract, like the opposite poles of a magnet. In the atom of any element, the number of protons is equal to the number of electrons. So the positive and negative charges balance each other.

It is the number of protons in an atom that determines what the element is. The elements found in nature can have as many as 92 protons. Hydrogen's atom, it turns out, is the simplest of all. It has only one proton and one electron. No wonder hydrogen weighs so little!

A proton weighs 1,836 times as much as an electron. So in a hydrogen atom, the proton is responsible for almost all the weight of the atom.

A simple way to picture a hydrogen atom is as a proton with an electron circling it as the Earth circles the Sun. To get an idea of the distances in the atom, imagine that the proton is about the same size as a basketball. The electron would be flying around it at a distance of 19 miles (almost 31 km) away! So you can see that hydrogen atoms—and all other atoms—are mostly empty space. Yet they are very small. They are so small that a sheet of paper, which has atoms of many different elements in it, is one million atoms thick.

Because it has only one proton and one electron, hydrogen is the smallest in size of all the atoms. As a matter of fact, it could not be used in some early balloons because of its tiny size. Its molecules could leak out through tiny holes between fibers in the balloon fabric.

HYDROGEN ATOM

lectron

Proton

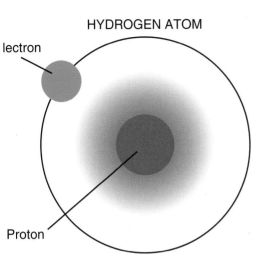
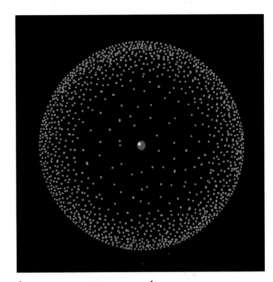

Hydrogen is usually pictured as an electron moving around a proton as shown to the left. But scientists believe that an electron really looks like a cloud around the proton as shown at right.

The little ghost can even pass through rubber, clay, and metal by sneaking between molecules! No other substance is able to do such an amazing thing.

Can you begin to see how the number of protons and electrons in an atom might determine an element's properties? The number of protons in the atoms of an element is called its *atomic number*. Scientists have organized the elements according to atomic number in a chart called the periodic table. With its one proton, hydrogen is number 1 in the table. Helium is number 2 because it has two protons, and lithium is number 3 because it has three protons. Oxygen, with eight protons, is number 8.

Periodic Table

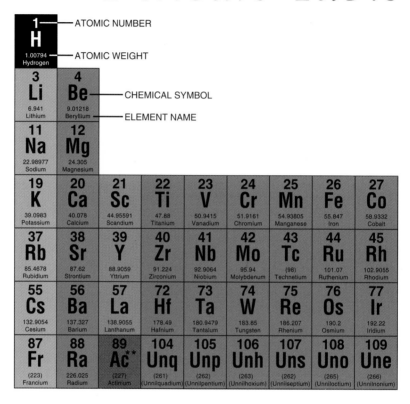

ATOMIC NUMBER

1
H
1.00794 — ATOMIC WEIGHT
Hydrogen

CHEMICAL SYMBOL

ELEMENT NAME

3 **Li** 6.941 Lithium	4 **Be** 9.01218 Beryllium							
11 **Na** 22.98977 Sodium	12 **Mg** 24.305 Magnesium							
19 **K** 39.0983 Potassium	20 **Ca** 40.078 Calcium	21 **Sc** 44.95591 Scandium	22 **Ti** 47.88 Titanium	23 **V** 50.9415 Vanadium	24 **Cr** 51.9161 Chromium	25 **Mn** 54.93805 Manganese	26 **Fe** 55.847 Iron	27 **Co** 58.9332 Cobalt
37 **Rb** 85.4678 Rubidium	38 **Sr** 87.62 Strontium	39 **Y** 88.9059 Yttrium	40 **Zr** 91.224 Zirconium	41 **Nb** 92.9064 Niobium	42 **Mo** 95.94 Molybdenum	43 **Tc** (98) Technetium	44 **Ru** 101.07 Ruthenium	45 **Rh** 102.9055 Rhodium
55 **Cs** 132.9054 Cesium	56 **Ba** 137.327 Barium	57 **La** 138.9055 Lanthanum	72 **Hf** 178.49 Hafnium	73 **Ta** 180.9479 Tantalum	74 **W** 183.85 Tungsten	75 **Re** 186.207 Rhenium	76 **Os** 190.2 Osmium	77 **Ir** 192.22 Iridium
87 **Fr** (223) Francium	88 **Ra** 226.025 Radium	89 **Ac**** (227) Actinium	104 **Unq** (261) (Unnilquadium)	105 **Unp** (262) (Unnilpentium)	106 **Unh** (263) (Unnilhoxium)	107 **Uns** (262) (Unnilseptium)	108 **Uno** (265) (Unniloctium)	109 **Une** (266) (Unnilnonium)

The elements are organized here according to atomic number, the number of protons in an atom of the element. Hydrogen, with atomic number 1, is the smallest and lightest of all the elements.

58 **Ce** 140.115 Cerium	59 **Pr** 140.9077 Praseodymium	60 **Nd** 144.24 Neodymium	61 **Pm** (145) Promethium	62 **Sm** 150.36 Samarium
90 **Th** 232.0381 Thorium	91 **Pa** 231.0359 Protactinium	92 **U** 238.029 Uranium	93 **Np** 237.048 Neptunium	94 **Pu** (244) Plutonium

of the Elements

								2 **He** 4.00260 Helium
		5 **B** 10.811 Boron	6 **C** 12.011 Carbon	7 **N** 14.067 Nitrogen	8 **O** 15.994 Oxygen	9 **F** 18.998403 Florine	10 **Ne** 20.1797 Neon
		13 **Al** 26.96154 Aluminum	14 **Si** 28.0855 Silicon	15 **P** 30.973762 Phosphorous	16 **S** 32.066 Sulfur	17 **Cl** 35.4527 Chlorine	18 **Ar** 39.948 Argon
28 **Ni** 58.693 Nickel	29 **Cu** 63.546 Copper	30 **Zn** 65.39 Zinc	31 **Ga** 69.723 Gallium	32 **Ge** 72.61 Germanium	33 **As** 72.9216 Arsenic	34 **Se** 78.96 Selenium	35 **Br** 79.904 Bromine	36 **Kr** 83.80 Krypton
46 **Pd** 106.42 Palladium	47 **Ag** 107.8682 Silver	48 **Cd** 112.41 Cadmium	49 **In** 114.82 Indium	50 **Sn** 118.71 Tin	51 **Sb** 121.757 Antimony	52 **Te** 127.60 Tellurium	53 **I** 126.9045 Iodine	54 **Xe** 131.29 Xenon
78 **Pt** 195.08 Platinum	79 **Au** 196.9665 Gold	80 **Hg** 200.59 Mercury	81 **Ti** 204.383 Thallium	82 **Pb** 207.2 Lead	83 **Bi** 208.9804 Bismuth	84 **Po** (209) Polonium	85 **At** (210) Astatine	86 **Rn** (222) Radon

63 **Eu** 151.965 Europium	64 **Gd** 157.25 Gadolinium	65 **Tb** 158.9253 Terbium	66 **Dy** 162.50 Dysprosium	67 **Ho** 164.9303 Holmium	68 **Er** 167.26 Erbium	69 **Tm** 168.9342 Thulium	70 **Yb** 173.04 Ytterbium	71 **Lu** 174.967 Lutetium
95 **Am** (243) Americium	96 **Cm** (247) Berkelium	97 **Bk** (247) Berkelium	98 **Cf** (251) Californium	99 **Es** (252) Einsteinium	100 **Fm** (257) Fermium	101 **Md** (258) Mendelevium	102 **No** (259) Nobelium	103 **Lr** (260) Lawrencium

Elements also have a third kind of particle that helps determine their properties. *Neutrons* are found with the protons in the *nucleus*, the center of the atom. Neutrons have no electric charge; they are neutral, which is how they got their name. Hydrogen is the only element that doesn't have any neutrons in its atomic nucleus.

But there are rare forms of hydrogen that do have neutrons. About one in a hundred hydrogen atoms have a neutron in the nucleus. This form of hydrogen is called *deuterium*. Because a neutron weighs a bit more than a proton, it weighs down the hydrogen atom a lot. So this form of hydrogen is sometimes called heavy hydrogen. Different forms of an element are called *isotopes*. Another isotope of hydrogen has two neutrons. It is called *tritium*. Deuterium and tritium have different properties than ordinary hydrogen, as you will see in Chapter 5.

With no neutrons, ordinary hydrogen is the lightest possible atom there is. We can be quite certain that scientists will never discover a lighter element. Hydrogen will always rise above the rest.

Chapter 4

BONDING WITH OTHERS

Hydrogen is one of the friendliest elements around. It bonds to more kinds of atoms than any other element except carbon. When hydrogen bonds with other elements, the resulting compounds look and act completely different from the invisible gas H_2. It's as if the little ghost were able to disguise itself by latching onto other elements.

You already know that the bonding of hydrogen to oxygen produces water. You may never have seen hydrogen, but you can see water practically everywhere. It is in oceans, lakes, and rivers; it is in our sinks and showers; and it is in our food and drink. We cannot live without it. Although most of the weight of water comes from oxygen, hydrogen makes water a very special liquid.

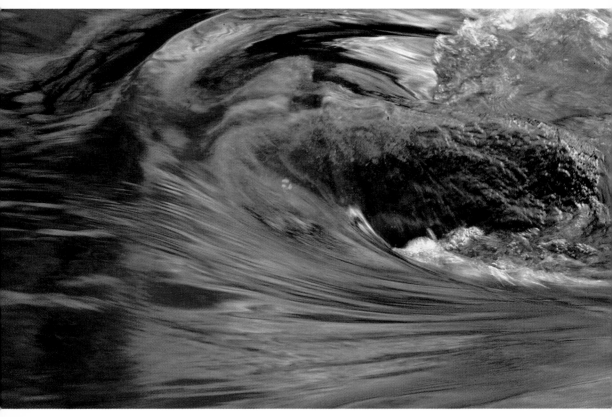

Water is the most important hydrogen compound.

To understand the reason for this, you must know how atoms bond together. Here is where electrons come into play. A hydrogen atom and an oxygen atom bond together so that they can share electrons with each other. Like people, electrons prefer to gather in groups, or families. In a single atom, the electrons closest to the nucleus form a family of two. If the atom has more electrons, they start a second family farther out from the nucleus. This second family always has eight electrons.

Oxygen, with a total of eight electrons, has a first family of two electrons, but only six electrons in its second family. It joins with two hydrogen atoms so that the two extra electrons can complete its second family. And hydrogen's single electrons are now part of a complete, happy family.

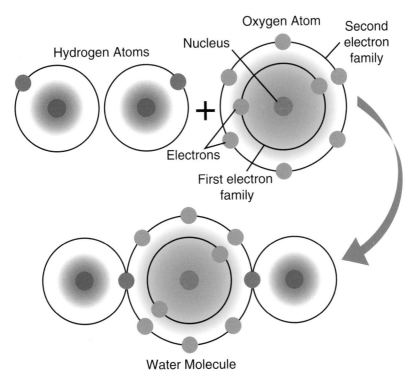

Two hydrogen atoms bond with an oxygen atom to form water.

If an atom of an element has complete families by itself, it does not bond with other atoms at all. Helium, for example, has a complete family of two electrons. It is called a "noble gas," as if it were too much of a snob to bond with other elements. But its snobbery made helium the ideal replacement for hydrogen in dirigibles. Since it refuses to react chemically with other elements, it cannot possibly go up in flames or explode.

HYDROGEN BONDS

One of the things that make water special is the position of the atoms in its molecule. Instead of forming a straight line, the hydrogen atoms sit at an angle to the oxygen atom. This means that one end of the molecule has a positive charge and the other end has a negative charge. The end containing the hydrogen atoms is positively charged because they lend their electrons to the oxygen atom. The extra electrons give the oxygen atom a negative charge.

So the negative, oxygen end of the molecule attracts a hydrogen atom from a nearby water molecule. This weak attraction is called a *hydrogen bond*. It causes the water molecules to stick together in a stiff pattern. In other liquids, the molecules are free to slide around each other in any way they wish.

Because water molecules are connected so stiffly, it takes high temperatures to melt ice and boil water. If it were not for the hydrogen bond, water would be a gas at

In a water molecule, the two hydrogen atoms are at an angle to the oxygen atom, as shown here. This makes water a very special liquid.

most temperatures on earth. How do scientists know this? Because there is a compound that's very similar to water, except that it has no hydrogen bonds between its molecules. This compound, which is called *hydrogen sulfide*, boils at -114°F (-81°C).

Hydrogen sulfide has two hydrogen atoms and one sulfur atom in its molecule, so its formula, H_2S, is a lot like water's. And sulfur, like oxygen, has six electrons in its outermost family. (But since sulfur has a total of sixteen electrons, it bonds with hydrogen to complete a *third* family of eight electrons.) As a result of these similarities, H_2S and H_2O have many of the same properties. But because there are no hydrogen bonds in hydrogen sulfide, it boils much more easily than water. If water were like that, you and I could not exist.

Lakes and oceans freeze first on top because of hydrogen bonds.
The bonds cause water to expand when it freezes
instead of contracting as other liquids do.

The hydrogen bonds in water do something else that's very important. They cause water to expand when it freezes, instead of contracting, as almost every other solid does. So water is less dense in its solid form than in its liquid form. That means ice floats on water instead of sinking to the bottom.

If ice sank in water, the world would be a very different place. Lakes and oceans would freeze from bottom to top in the winter, killing all the plants and animals that live in them. In our world, when water begins to freeze, it expands and rises before it gets a chance to completely freeze. The water on top of a lake or ocean may freeze, but plants and animals can still live under the ice.

ACIDS AND BASES

Another interesting thing about water is that it is both an *acid* and a *base*. Acids are sour-tasting chemicals that in some cases can eat through substances. The *ascorbic acid* in orange juice and lemon juice is mild and harmless; in fact, it's Vitamin C. But *hydrochloric acid*, which is the acid Robert Boyle mixed with iron, is very dangerous.

The first thing you'll notice about acids is that almost all of them contain hydrogen. Hydrochloric acid, or HCl, has one hydrogen atom and one *chlorine* atom. The chlorine atom has seven electrons in its outer family so only one hydrogen electron is needed to complete it.

When HCl is dissolved in water, the hydrogen atom leaves its electron with the chlorine atom and roams the water freely. Without its electron, it is really only a proton, which has a positive electric charge. The chlorine atom has an extra electron, so it has a negative charge. These charged particles are called hydrogen and chlorine *ions*. The more hydrogen ions floating freely in an acid, the more acidic it is.

In a way, bases are the opposite of acids. When you add a little base to an acid, it becomes less acidic. That's because bases bond with the hydrogen ions, removing them from the solution.

Bases taste bitter rather than sour. A weak base you can usually find around the house is baking soda. Another example of a base is *sodium hydroxide*, which has a formula of NaOH. Na is the symbol for the element *sodium*. When the base is dissolved in water, the sodium atom donates its one outer electron to the OH pair of atoms. That gives the pair a negative charge. These negative OH pairs make the solution basic, they combine with hydrogen ions to form water.

If HCl and NaOH are combined, the reaction produces water and NaCl—sodium chloride, which is table salt. Chemists write this reaction as:

$$HCl + NaOH = NaCl + H_2O$$

Water has both positive hydrogen ions and negative OH pairings. So it is the only substance that is both an acid and a base.

OTHER COMPOUNDS

Because hydrogen has only one electron, it is welcomed by many families. No matter how many electrons a family needs, hydrogen can fill the empty slots, even if it takes three or more hydrogen atoms to do it. Some elements couldn't fill the bill, no matter how many of them there are. Chlorine, for example, never combines with oxygen because they both need only an electron or two to complete their outer families.

Hydrogen is an important part of *organic compounds*. They are compounds containing carbon, and many of them are found in living tissue. Hydrogen bonds help hold proteins in unusual shapes that are critical to performing their duties in the body. In fat tissue, the amount of hydrogen determines how solid it is. The more hydrogen, the more solid the fat. Food companies add hydrogen to vegetable oils to make them solid like butter. This is margarine, which some people use instead of butter.

Because hydrogen is added to it, margarine is called a *hydrogenated fat*. Butter and the fat in animals contains *cholesterol*, another organic compound with a lot of hydrogen atoms. Many health experts believe it is not good to eat a lot of solid fat and cholesterol. If cholesterol builds up too much in blood vessels, it can cause heart problems.

But there is a good reason for hydrogen to be in fat and oil. Whenever your body needs energy, it *metabolizes*, or breaks down, some of the fat. It snips the hydrogen atoms from the carbon atoms, and when these atoms form new bonds, energy is released. Hydrogen bonds with oxygen and forms water. Every time this happens, you have more energy to run and jump and shout.

Another important hydrogen compound is ammonia. Most of the hydrogen produced in the world today is used to make ammonia. You probably know ammonia as a powerful cleaner that doesn't smell so great. But ammonia is actually a compound containing hydrogen and nitrogen. Nitrogen is an element that is the main gas in air. Its atom has five electrons in its outer family, and it bonds with three hydrogen atoms to make an ammonia molecule. The formula for ammonia is NH_3.

So hydrogen is not only in your food and drink and in your bath and shower. It is most likely in your bathroom cleaner, too. It's even inside you. The little ghost is in disguise all around us, hiding in many places.

Chapter 5

THE POWER OF HYDROGEN

When Robert Boyle set hydrogen on fire in the seventeenth century, he saw it burn with a greenish-blue flame. But hydrogen's flame, like the little ghost itself, is really invisible. Boyle's flame was probably colored by particles in the air burning with the hydrogen. Even though burning hydrogen is invisible, it gives off more heat than a wood fire does.

The heat comes from the bonding of hydrogen and oxygen atoms. Whenever atoms bond together, they give off energy. People have wondered for a long time whether hydrogen could be burned to generate lots of energy. If so, it could replace coal, oil, and natural gas. They are the main sources of heat and electricity in the world today.

Burning hydrogen has no color, but a little bit of methane
was added to this hydrogen flame to make it blue.
The reddish color is hot steam forming.

When these fuels burn, they give off gases that pollute the air. But hydrogen's invisible flame doesn't pollute the air. As you know, when you burn hydrogen, all you get is water. Hydrogen could also be burned like gasoline to make a car go. Car makers, such as Daimler-Benz, have built trucks and buses that run on hydrogen. The only thing that comes out of the tailpipe is water!

But engineers haven't solved other problems with using hydrogen as a fuel. Since hydrogen gas takes up so much space, not much of it would fit in a gasoline tank. To get enough of it in a tank, it would have to be cooled and squeezed until it shrinks into a liquid.

And there would have to be a lot of extra equipment on the engine to keep the hydrogen liquid. This kind of engine is too heavy and too expensive to sell, the carmakers say. Another problem is that right now there are no filling stations that sell hydrogen. There are similar problems in using hydrogen to generate heat and electricity. Large amounts of liquid hydrogen fuel would have to be stored and moved from place to place.

But some people think the only real problem with hydrogen is that people are afraid of it because of the *Hindenburg* disaster. They are still hoping that we will someday get most of our energy from the invisible flame.

One way hydrogen is being used now is to fuel rockets. It is stored as a liquid so that it is compact and light. Yet hydrogen can generate the great power needed to lift rockets and shuttles into space.

STAR POWER

Space seems to be the place where hydrogen is most at home. Most of what we see in outer space—the stars and the galaxies—is made of hydrogen. That's something astronomers have just discovered in this century. Even

Hydrogen fuel powers the space shuttle. You can see hydrogen's clear flames to the right, coming out of the shuttle itself.

though hydrogen accounts for only 0.9 percent of the weight of everything on Earth, it makes up about 75 percent of stars like the Sun.

Astronomers believe that stars form when incredible forces of gravity pull huge clouds of hydrogen gas into swirls. The hydrogen becomes denser and denser and its atoms become packed together very hard. Think about squeezing a handful of snow harder and harder, until you have a very small, heavy snowball.

The force of gravity in stars is so strong that the protons in the hydrogen atoms almost touch. Protons normally push away from each other because they have the same positive electric charge. But when they're forced together by immense gravity, the atoms fuse to create a new nucleus. This nuclear reaction, called *fusion*, releases tremendous amounts of energy in an explosion. It is different from a chemical reaction because the bonding takes place between protons, not electrons.

The explosions of hydrogen in the Sun are so powerful that it is difficult for us to imagine them. Temperatures can reach as high as 25 million$^{\circ}$F (almost 14 million$^{\circ}$C). That is why we can see the light and feel the warmth of the Sun from many millions of miles away. So both sunlight and starlight come from hydrogen. The little ghost is even more powerful than Cavendish and Lavoisier ever dreamed!

When the protons fuse together, one of them loses its electric charge and becomes a neutron. You may recall

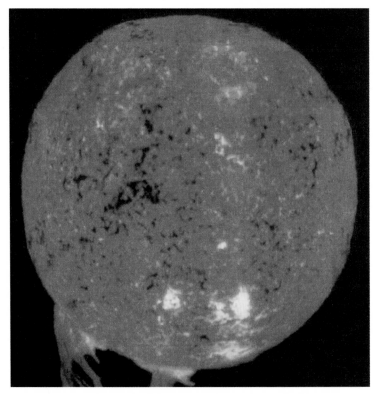

Hydrogen is the fuel of the Sun and other stars. But instead of burning as in the shuttle, the hydrogen atoms fuse together, releasing tremendous amounts of energy.

from Chapter 3 that an atom with one proton and one neutron is a form of hydrogen called deuterium.

Another, more powerful fusion reaction can take place between a deuterium atom and a tritium atom. When they fuse, they produce a completely new element—helium.

Helium has two protons and two neutrons. A third, left-over neutron flies off by itself. In this fusion reaction, it takes only 1 pound (almost 0.5 kg) of hydrogen to release as much energy as *6 million* pounds (*2.7 million* kg) of burning gasoline.

Believe it or not, 650 million tons of hydrogen fuse into helium in the Sun every *second*. Even so, the Sun has enough hydrogen to keep burning for eight billion more years.

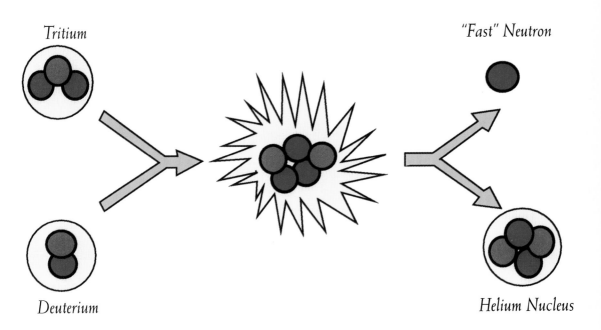

Tritium

"Fast" Neutron

Deuterium

Helium Nucleus

One kind of fusion process joins a nucleus of tritium with a nucleus of deuterium. The neutrons are shown in blue and the protons in red.

BACK TO WAR

Scientists were realizing how powerful nuclear reactions could be around the beginning of World War II. A group of scientists working for the Germans on one side and another working for the United States on the other raced to put that power into a bomb. The American group won the race. The first bomb they invented worked by splitting atoms of an element called *uranium* into atoms of two lighter elements. This type of nuclear reaction, called *fission*, releases enormous energy.

During the war, the United States dropped two of these fission bombs on Japan. The bombs caused many deaths and terrible destruction. One bomb destroyed two thirds of the city of Hiroshima. But some people believe the bombs brought the war with Japan to a speedy end and saved lives.

Scientists knew that fusion bombs using hydrogen would have even greater explosive power than uranium bombs. Americans tested an early version of the hydrogen bomb, or H-bomb, in 1952 on an island called Eniwetok in the Pacific Ocean.

The scientists nicknamed the bomb "Mike." To keep it compact, the hydrogen was stored as a liquid. With all the cooling equipment needed to keep the hydrogen liquid, the bomb weighed 82 tons. When it exploded, the bomb created a mushroom-shaped cloud. The force of the bomb made a crater more than a mile (almost 2 km) wide and 164 feet (50 m) deep.

*The first hydrogen bomb, named "Mike," was tested
in the Pacific Ocean. The little ghost turned out
to be more powerful than anyone ever dreamed.*

In March 1954, the United States tested another
hydrogen weapon on the Bikini atoll, an island in the
Pacific Ocean. The radiation from the bomb accidentally
contaminated Japanese fishermen at sea. Many of them
became sick. The fishermen complained that the bomb
had killed fish as well. After that, the United States and

other countries began testing the bombs deep underground, to avoid hurting people and animals.

Today most nuclear weapons are hydrogen bombs. They have much greater explosive force than the bombs dropped on Japan. The H-bomb dropped on the Bikini atoll was 1,000 times more powerful than the fission bomb dropped on Hiroshima. That H-bomb created 15 *megatons* of explosive force. A megaton is the amount of force produced by 1,000,000 tons of TNT. Bombs as big as 50 megatons have been tested by both the Soviet Union (now Russia and other countries) and the United States.

But scientists have also been working to develop hydrogen fusion for a peaceful purpose. They are trying to figure out a way to tame this furious power so that it can generate electricity. The heat from the fusing of atoms could boil water, and the steam could then run electric generators.

Like power from burning hydrogen, hydrogen fusion would not pollute the atmosphere. And it would not produce the nuclear waste that today's nuclear power plants do. Today's plants generate nuclear power from fission, the splitting of uranium atoms. In fusion, there would be no nuclear waste and no harmful radiation released.

The result of the fusion reaction is only snobby helium, which you've already read is very safe. It doesn't bond with anything or hurt anyone. But before we can get safe energy from hydrogen, scientists must understand fusion better. They don't yet know how to control the reaction once it starts.

Lasers can create hydrogen fusion in the laboratory.

Learning about fusion is also helping scientists understand how our universe came about. Stars generate heavier elements by the fusion of larger and larger atoms. Like big element factories, stars churn out many different elements. But it all started with hydrogen. Hydrogen was undoubtedly the first element to be born in the universe.

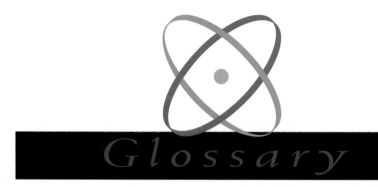

Glossary

absolute zero—the lowest temperature possible. It is $-459^{\circ}F$ $(-273^{\circ}C)$. Atoms, which normally vibrate, stop moving at this temperature.

acid—a sour-tasting group of chemical compounds. Almost all acids contain hydrogen ions that have given up their electrons. The positive hydrogen ions give these compounds their acidity. Acids react chemically with bases to produce salts and water.

ascorbic acid—an acid found in fruits and vegetables. It is also known as Vitamin C.

atomic number—the number of protons in an element's atom. Since each element has a different number of protons in its atom, the atomic number identifies the element. Hydrogen's atomic number is 1.

base—a bitter-tasting group of chemical compounds. Most of them contain pairs of oxygen and hydrogen atoms bonded together with an extra electron. It is these negatively charged pairs that make them bases. Bases react chemically with acids to produce salts and water.

chemical reaction—a process in which atoms bond together or break apart. Two or more elements may join to create a compound, or a compound may break down into its elements. Hydrogen burning in air, for example, is a chemical reaction in which hydrogen atoms bond with oxygen atoms. The substances before the reaction have different properties than the substances after the reaction.

chemist—a scientist who studies materials and how they interact with each other.

chlorine—a greenish-yellow gas with a strong odor. It is one of the elements.

cholesterol—a substance in animals that is part of body fat.

compound—a substance made up of two or more elements chemically bonded together.

density—a measure of how closely packed a substance is with matter. It is calculated by dividing the weight or mass of a substance by the amount of space it takes up.

deuterium—an isotope of hydrogen with one neutron. It weighs twice as much as ordinary hydrogen and is also known as heavy hydrogen.

dirigible—an airship; a flying balloon that can be steered and propelled.

electron—a tiny particle in an atom. It has a negative charge and makes it possible for atoms to bonds with one another.

element—one of 92 substances that make up everything in the world. About 20 more elements have been made artificially in laboratories. An element contains only one kind of atom and cannot be broken down into any simpler substance.

fission—the splitting of an atomic nucleus. This nuclear process releases so much energy that it can be used in bombs. The first atomic bombs were fission bombs.

fusion—the joining of protons of one atom with the protons of another atom. Because this process releases tremendous energy, it is used in bombs. Fusion also generates energy in the Sun and stars.

gas—a substance that has no definite shape or volume, but spreads into whatever space is available. It is the form a substance takes when the temperature of its liquid form is raised so high that its molecules rise into the air. The "gas" people put in their cars is something else entirely; it is the liquid *gasoline*, which is sometimes called *gas* for short.

helium—an invisible gas used in balloons and blimps. It is a chemical element that is inert; it does not bond with other elements.

hydrochloric acid—a strong acid used in industry. In a weak, diluted form, it also helps digest food in the stomach.

hydrogen bond—a weak bond between molecules caused by hydrogen atoms at one end of each molecule. Since the hydrogen atoms have positive charges, one end of the molecule is positively charged and the other end is negatively charged. As a result, the molecules are attracted to each other and line up in a stiff pattern.

hydrogen sulfide—a poisonous gas that smells like rotten eggs.

hydrogenated fat—an oil that has hydrogen atoms added to it to make it solid.

ion—an atom that has an electric charge because it has given electrons to other atoms or because it has taken electrons from other atoms.

isotope—one of two or more forms of an element. Isotopes have similar properties, but different weights because they have different numbers of neutrons.

matter—anything that takes up space and has mass.

megaton—a unit of measure that specifies the amount of explosive force in a powerful bomb. A megaton is equal to the explosive force produced by 1 million tons of TNT.

metabolize—to break down food in the body for energy. Metabolism is a chemical reaction in which bonds are broken and new ones are formed. Energy is released when the new bonds form.

molecule—two or more atoms bonded together to form a compound. Molecules can sometimes form in elements too, as when hydrogen atoms bond in pairs in hydrogen gas.

neutron—a particle in the center, or nucleus. of an atom. It has no electric charge. It changes the mass of an element. Different numbers of neutrons in the nucleus create different isotopes of the element.

nitrogen—an invisible gas that makes up 78 percent of air. It is a chemical element.

nucleus—the center of an atom. It contains protons and neutrons.

organic compound—a chemical containing carbon. Most organic compounds also contain hydrogen, and many are found in living things.

oxygen—an invisible gas that makes up 21 percent of air. It is a chemical element, and animals need it to live.

property—a quality or a behavior that a substance displays.

proton—a particle in the center, or nucleus, of an atom. It has a positive electric charge. The number of protons determines which element the atom is.

sodium—a silvery white, soft element.

sodium hydroxide—a white solid that is used to make soap. It is a base.

tritium—an isotope of hydrogen containing two neutrons. It weighs three times as much as ordinary hydrogen.

uranium—a very heavy element. The atomic nuclei of uranium are split in fission bombs.

volume—an amount of space, such as a quart or a liter.

zeppelin—an airship developed by a German company around 1900 to carry passengers to their destinations. It was shaped like a large whale.

Sources

Brock, William H. *The Norton History of Chemistry*. New York: W.W. Norton & Company, 1992.

Glines, C.V., ed. *Lighter-Than-Air Flight*. New York: Franklin Watts, 1965.

Hoffman, Peter. *The Forever Fuel: The Story of Hydrogen*. Boulder, Colorado: Westview Press, 1981.

Hudson, John. *The History of Chemistry*. New York: Routledge, Chapman, & Hall, 1992.

McGowen, Tom. *Chemistry: The Birth of a Science*. New York: Franklin Watts, 1989.

Mooney, Michael M. *The Hindenburg*. New York: Dodd, Mead, & Company, 1972.

Newton, David E. *The Chemical Elements*. New York: Franklin Watts, 1994.

Weeks, Mary Elvira. *Discovery of the Elements*. Easton, Pennsylvania: Journal of Chemical Education, 1968.

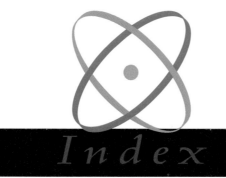

Index

Italicized page numbers
indicate illustrations.

About the Author

Mark D. Uehling has a master's degree in journalism from Columbia University. He has written about technology and the environment for publications such as *Popular Science, Chicago,* and *The New York Times.* He has worked on the staffs of *Newsweek* and *The Sciences,* a publication of the New York Academy of Sciences. He lives in Chicago.